THE
ARAN
ISLANDS

The Curriculum Development Unit (CDU)

The CDU, established in 1972 by the City of Dublin Vocational Education Committee (CDVEC), Trinity College Dublin, and the Department of Education and Science, is a curriculum research and development institute which, over the years, has initiated a variety of projects and courses at primary and post-primary (junior and senior cycle), further and adult education and in youth and community provision. For more information, see www.curriculum.ie.

This book was researched and edited by Paul O'Sullivan, with revisions by Nora Godwin.

THE
ARAN
ISLANDS
AT THE EDGE OF THE WORLD

THE O'BRIEN PRESS
DUBLIN

This updated and revised edition first published 2017 by
The O'Brien Press Ltd,
12 Terenure Road East, Rathgar, Dublin 6, D06 HD27, Ireland.
Tel: +353 1 4923333; Fax: +353 1 4922777
E-mail: books@obrien.ie; Website: www.obrien.ie
First published as *A World of Stone: Life, Folklore and Legends of the Aran Islands* by O'Brien Educational in 1977.
Republished as *The Aran Islands: A World of Stone* by The O'Brien Press in 2003.
Reprinted 1980 (twice), 1982, 1985, 1988, 1991, 2003, 2008.
The O'Brien Press is a member of Publishing Ireland.

ISBN: 978-1-84717-867-1

8 7 6 5 4 3 2 1
21 20 19 18 17

Editing, typesetting, layout and design: The O'Brien Press Ltd
Printed and bound in Poland by Białostockie Zakłady Graficzne S.A.
The paper in this book is produced using pulp from managed forests.

Published in:

DUBLIN

UNESCO
City of Literature

CONTENTS

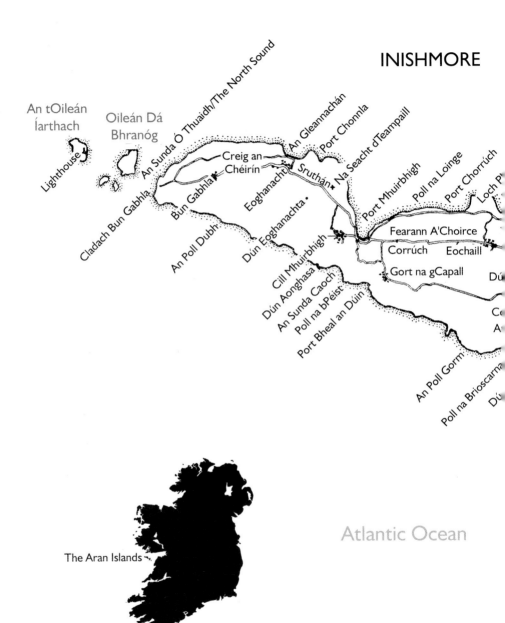

INISHMORE

An tOileán Íarthach

Oileán Dá Bhranóg

Lighthouse

An Sunda Ó Thuaidh/The North Sound

An Gleannachán

Port Chonnla

Na Seacht dTeampaill

Creig an Chéirín

Eoghanacht

Sruthán

Port Muirbhigh

Poll na Loinge

Port Chorrúch

Loch P

Cladach Bun Gabhla

Bun Gabhla

An Poll Dubh

Dún Eoghanachta

Eoghanachta

Fearann A'Choirce

Corrúch

Eochaill

Cill Mhuirbhigh

Dún Aonghasa

An Sunda Caoch

Poll na bPéist

Port Bheal an Dúin

Gort na gCapall

Dú

C

A

An Poll Gorm

Poll na Brioscarna

Dú

The Aran Islands

Atlantic Ocean

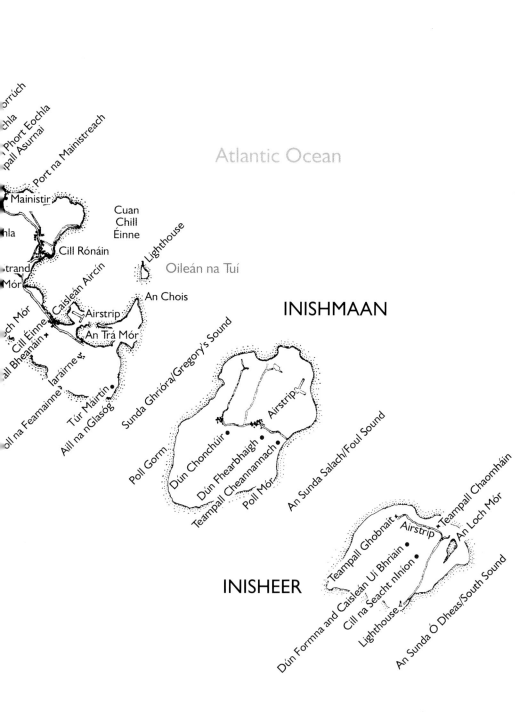

orrúch

chla

Phort Eochla

pall Asurnaí

Port na Mainistreach

Atlantic Ocean

Mainistir

Cuan
Chill
Éinne

hla

Lighthouse

Cill Rónáin

Oileán na Tuí

trand

Mór

Caisleán Aircín

An Chois

Loch Mór

Airstrip

Cill Éinne

An Trá Mór

all Bheanáin

Iaráirne

Túr Máirtín

Aill na nGlasóg

ll na Feamainne

INISHMAAN

Sunda Ghrióra/Gregory's Sound

Airstrip

Poll Gorm

Dún Chonchúir

Dún Fhearbhaigh

An Sunda Salach/Foul Sound

Teampall Cheannannach

Poll Mór

Teampall Chaomháin

Airstrip

An Loch Mór

Teampall Ghobnait

Caisleán Uí Bhriain

Dún Formna and

Cill na Seacht nIníon

INISHEER

Lighthouse

An Sunda Ó Dheas/South Sound

From Doonagore Castle in County Clare, a view of the 'three stepping stones out of Europe', the Aran Islands.

CHAPTER ONE

DISCOVERING ARAN

'The Evening Land'
By Seamus Heaney

From Connemara, or the Moher clifftop,
Where the land ends with a sheer drop,
You can see three stepping stones out of Europe.

Anchored like hulls at the dim horizon
Against the winds' and the waves' explosion.

The Aran Islands are all awash.
East coastline's furled in the foam's white sash.
The clouds melt over them like slush.

And on Galway Bay, between shore and shore,
The ferry plunges to Aranmore.

The Aran Islands are a group of windswept, grey rock ledges off the west coast of Ireland. Creeping one by one away from the Connacht mainland, and facing the open Atlantic, they harbour memories of ancient Ireland, the history and traditions of Gaelic culture, and the spirit, songs and stories of an island people.

The three main islands, Inishmore, Inishmaan and Inisheer, are long and low, resembling a group of stranded whales, and together they extend over twenty-five kilometres in an almost perfectly straight line across the mouth of Galway Bay. About 1,250 people live on the islands, but in the summer season visitors swell the numbers considerably.

The Aran Islands are a native Gaeltacht, in which the Irish language is the predominant vernacular or language of the home. The name Aran may have been derived from the Irish word *ara*, which means 'kidney', because of the kidney shape of Inishmore. It equally may have been abbreviated from the Irish expression *ard-thuinn*, meaning 'the height of the waves'. According to legend, the islands are the remnants of a rock barrier that once stretched from Galway to Clare, trapping the waters of the present Galway Bay in a gigantic lake. All three islands are alike in their rock base and also similar to the nearby Burren on the north Clare mainland.

Inisheer (*Inis Oírr*: the Eastern Island) is the nearest to County Clare, lying just under ten kilometres north-west of Doolin. It is the smallest of Aran's three main islands, almost square in shape, with an area of ten square kilometres. The broad sweep of the South Sound isolates Inisheer from the mainland, and boats cross regularly from Doolin.

Inishmaan (*Inis Meáin*: the Middle Island) is the next along, separated from Inisheer by three kilometres of water known as Foul Sound. On the

The wind-swept cliffs of Inishmore, the largest Aran island.

other side, it is separated from Inishmore by two kilometres of open sea known as Gregory's Sound, named after a revered hermit saint, Gregory of the Golden Mouth, who is reputed to have lived and died on Inishmaan. It is much smaller than Inishmore and more compact in shape, extending just five kilometres from east to west.

Inishmore (*Inis Mór*: the Big Island) lies nearest to the Galway mainland and is the largest and best-known island. It is regarded as the 'capital' of the Aran Islands. The sheltered harbour at Kilronan (*Cill Rónáin*) has long been the main entry point for visitors to Aran. The island's inhabitants occupy an area amounting to little more than thirty-one

A patchwork of small fields on Inishmaan.

kilometres. The bay of Killeany (*Cill Éinne*) forms a natural 'waist' to the island. From there, Inishmore rises north-westward and achieves its greatest width before descending to the narrow 'neck' at Port Murvey (*Port Mhuirbhigh*), less than a kilometre wide. A second, slightly lower ridge rises to the west of this bay, widening the island once more before it slopes gently down to the Atlantic at its north-western tip.

Other small, uninhabited islands complete the Aran group: Rock Island and Straw Island, both home to lighthouses; and Brannock Island (*Oileán dá Bhranóg*: the island of the two small ravens).

Nowadays, the Aran Islands are easily accessible by sea and air. Ferries run from Doolin in County Clare (seasonal) and Rossaveal in County Galway (all year round). Aer Arann Islands operates flights from Inverin in Galway to all three islands. But in times past, isolation was a feature of Aran life. Gale-force winds still occasionally sever shipping links, and back when this was the only form of transport, the population would have been cut off from the outside world, often for weeks on end. The shelving sea bed around the islands makes for a particularly treacherous sea during a storm – the waves break more than a kilometre from the shore, sending gigantic white combers rushing towards the rocks. Communications were then cut off, mail and visitors failed to arrive, and supplies of food ran low – the community had to rely on its own resources. If one of the inhabitants fell ill during storm conditions and needed hospitalisation, sometimes a crossing had to be attempted. The islanders grimly joked that a patient, in his terror, forgot about his illness until he reached the safety of Rossaveal on the mainland, where his condition immediately deteriorated once more!

Above: Traditional currachs. **Below:** The *Naomh Éanna* ferry sailed for thirty years between Galway and the Aran Islands, before it was taken out of action in 1986.

The Journey to Aran in the Nineteenth and Early Twentieth Centuries

In those years, travel to the islands was usually undertaken in the traditional *currach* (pr: cur-rock) or curragh, a boat made of skin fixed over a wooden frame, thus giving a light but fragile vessel that pitched and tossed with the high waves. What was it like to travel out to Aran this way? Here we have a description from John Millington Synge, the famous playwright, who visited Aran every summer from 1898 to 1902, living with families on Inishmore and Inishmaan. His book *The Aran Islands* is an account of life in that era.

We set off. It was a four-oared curragh, and I was given the last seat so as to leave the stern for the man who was steering with an oar, worked at right angles to the others by an extra thole-pin in the stern gunnel.

When we had gone about a hundred yards they ran up a bit of a sail in the bow and the pace became extraordinarily rapid.

The shower had passed over and the wind had fallen, but large magnificently brilliant waves were rolling down on us at right angles to our course.

Every instant the steersman whirled us round with a sudden stroke of his oar, the prow reared up and then fell into the next furrow with a crash, throwing up masses of spray. As it did so, the stern in its turn was thrown up, and both the steersman, who let go his oar and clung with both hands to the gunnel, and myself, were lifted high above the sea.

The wave passed, we regained our course and rowed violently for a few yards, when the same manoeuvre had to be repeated. As we worked out into the sound we began to meet another class of waves, that could be seen from some distance towering above the rest.

When one of these came in sight, the first effort was to get beyond its reach. The steersman began crying out in Gaelic '*Siubhal, siubhal*' ('Run, run'), and sometimes, when the mass was gliding towards us with horrible speed, his voice rose to a shriek. Then the rowers themselves took up the cry, and the curragh seemed to leap and quiver with the frantic terror of a beast till the wave passed behind it or fell with a crash beside the stern.

It was in this racing with the waves that our chief danger lay. If the wave could be avoided, it was better to do so, but if it overtook us while we were trying to escape, and caught us on the broadside, our destruction was certain. I could see the steersman quivering with the excitement of his task, for any error in his judgement would have swamped us.

We had one narrow escape. A wave appeared high above the rest, and there was the usual moment of intense exertion. It was of no use, and in an instant the wave seemed to be hurling itself upon us. With a yell of rage the steersman struggled with his oar to bring our prow to meet it. He had almost succeeded, when there was a crash and rush of water round us. I felt as if I had been struck on the back with knotted ropes. White foam gurgled round my knees and eyes. The curragh reared up, swaying and trembling for a moment, then fell safely into the furrow.

This was our worst moment, though more than once, when several waves came so closely together that we had no time to regain control of the canoe between them, we had some dangerous work. Our lives depended upon the skill and courage of the men, as the life of the rider or swimmer is often in his own hands, and the excitement of the struggle was too great to allow time for fear.

I enjoyed the passage. Down in this shallow trough of canvas that bent and trembled with the motion of the men, I had a far more intimate feeling of the glory and power of the waves than I have ever known in a steamer.

Even for the modern visitor, the sea journey from Rossaveal to Inishmore, which takes around forty minutes, is an unforgettable experience. The sweeping curve of Galway Bay recedes as the boat plunges towards a rocky outcrop that seems devoid of life: no trees, few visible buildings, stark cliffs. As the boat approaches its destination, the twin humps of Inishmore, often blurred by mist or haze, assume a more distinct outline. The grey uniformity of the surface rock is the dominant colour, and only

The Aran Islands passenger ferry leaving Doolin in County Clare.

gradually does the observer pick out the golden sandy beaches flecked with the white froth of the breaking waves. A little higher on the slopes the white-washed and grey-washed houses take shape, straggling in an irregular line along the leeside of the ridge. The ferry rounds the point of Straw Island (*Oileán na Tuí*) and Kilronan Harbour is now visible, fishing craft in their berths, or at anchor, and the muddle of people and activity on the pier.

One can only wonder what instinct brought the first people to Aran's shores. Then, the islands must have looked inhospitable and barren, certainly not attractive, to those seeking shelter, warmth and a life lived off the fat of the land. But to our hardy ancestors, the islands spoke of refuge from attackers, secure land that could be easily defended from all sides, and, of course, unparalleled staging posts in the trade routes that circumnavigated Ireland's coasts.

'Inisheer'
By Seamus Heaney

We first drop anchor, beyond the pier,
Off the first island called Inisheer,
Where all the islandmen and women
Wear bright-knit shawls and well-patched homespun,
The women with rainbows round their shoulders,
The oarsmen strong and grey as boulders.
The currachs that lie along the strand
Are hoisted up. Black new moons walk the sand
And down where the waves break in white lace,
The bobbing boats all plunge and race
And row right under the steamer's bows –
Then back they ride with homely cargoes.

The trip from the Inishmore pier to Dun Aengus is one of the most popular cycling routes in Ireland.

Today Aran is a holiday destination for a huge number of visitors each year. Much has changed here, but much has remained the same. Irish is still the first language of the islands, although the residents are now bilingual. Flocks of guillemots and herring gulls still nest in the cliffs, raising their cries to rival the voice of the wind. The waves still crash against the shore, sculpting new features and flinging seaweed far up the beach. And the people still tell stories of the past on wintry nights when the Atlantic rages, permitting no one to leave and no one to arrive. On Aran, the past and the present are intimately bound together, creating a historical record that is unique in Europe. These islands have much to teach us.

LIA ÁRANN
STONECRAFT

A shop selling jewellery, art and souvenirs in Kilmurvey Craft Village, Inishmore.

Modern houses on Inisheer.

CHAPTER TWO

THE TRADITIONAL LIFESTYLE

OF THE ARAN ISLANDERS

Because they were islanders, the people of Aran lived a unique, largely self-contained lifestyle, and were almost self-sufficient in terms of food, supplies, culture and entertainment. This way of life lasted well into the twentieth century, and elements still survive today. The census of 1901 gave the population of the islands as 2,845; it would steadily decline over the next century, falling under 2,000 by the 1940s and under 1,500 by the 1970s. (The most recent figures give the year-round population as about 1,250.) It was to be a century of change for the Aran Islands, and of rediscovery too, thanks to a renewed interest in Gaelic culture and history. Until recent times, Aran still relied on the ways of old and was very much a traditional Irish rural settlement. Life was difficult and demanding for the islanders – they worked long, hard hours trying to eke out a living from inhospitable soil.

A typical Aran farm cluster of the late nineteenth century.

WHERE PEOPLE LIVED: VILLAGES

The farm cluster, or *clachán* (pr: clah-hawn), was once the main type of settlement on the Aran Islands. Referred to locally as a 'village', the clachán
comprised a group of farmers' dwelling houses and outbuildings built close
together. It contrasted strongly with the dispersed form of settlement found
on the mainland, where each dwelling house stood at the centre of its own
farm, often a mile or more from its nearest neighbour. A typical clachán,
on the other hand, contained two to fifteen houses irregularly grouped
together. This type of settlement has its roots in Irish history, going back
almost to Celtic times, and clacháns were common in many parts of Ireland
before the Great Famine of the 1840s. Living close together gave people
a sense of security and solidarity. In the nineteenth century, the clachán
would not have had a main street, village green or market place, and would

have been without services such as a shop, pub, church or school, which is very different from the modern villages on Aran.

The clachán was a concrete expression of the close blood and marriage links that existed on the islands. For example, the surname Hernon embraced the majority of those living in Kilmurvey; Cooke was similarly associated with Bun Gowla, and Gill with Killeany. Where related families lived in close proximity, they were able to aid one another in their daily work, or in a crisis. The giving of *cabhair* (pr: cower), or help – often called 'cooring' – depended not on the payment of money for work performed but rather on a return of the favour at an appropriate time. Tasks requiring a large number of workers, such as harvesting rye or burning kelp, were carried out this way. A group of workers like this was known as a *meitheal* (pr: meh-hill). The giving and receiving of such help in this manner is part of life on Aran even to this day.

Almost all of the Aran clusters are located to the north, or leeside, of the slopes, as protection from prevailing winds was essential. The exception, Gort na gCapall ('the Field of the Horses'), is situated in the low neck of land between the two ridges of Inishmore, where it is exposed to the elements. Other than in the case of Gort na gCapall, the clusters are found on one of the two broad terraces midway between summit and shore. These broad limestone terraces are backed by thick bands of shale, and each is well watered by springs. The limited number of springs available on Aran is another reason for the clustering of houses. No dwellings are located on the crags at the back of the islands, though a shed or barn can be seen in some isolated fields.

In the post-Famine period, many of the clusters shrank; some, like Ballindun on Inishmaan, were reduced to just two occupied houses. But with the passage of time, many clusters have again been 'stretched' as new houses are built along the road. Inishmaan, viewed from the sea, presents a continuous line of houses rather than distinct villages. The number of villages on Inishmore varies from ten to fourteen, depending on whether one regards the smaller clusters as being independent of, or merged with, the larger ones. On Aran, settlement has tended to move downslope. New houses are generally taller than the old ones, and their builders seek a lower, more sheltered site. The houses in the village of Sruthán on Inishmore were all sited above the road in pre-Famine days, but the whole village is now situated below the road.

The natural rock formation of Poll na bPéist on Inishmore, pictured during the Red Bull Cliff Diving series.

Kilronan, the main settlement on Inishmore.

Killeany and Kilronan, both on Inishmore, are larger than the other Aran settlements and have a wider range of functions than the traditional clacháns. Killeany grew up around the fourteenth-century Franciscan friary and Arkyne's Castle (*Caisleán Aircín*). Its sheltered harbour, protected by the castle, made it the 'capital' of the islands for centuries. In its early days, Killeany's inhabitants were soldiers, sailors and government officials rather than farmers. They were divorced from the land, as was the fishing community that grew up around its harbour. The fort and its garrison have long since gone, but the people of Killeany are still less tied to the land than the other islanders. Kilronan resulted from the merging of two farm clusters along the main road early in the nineteenth century. After the Famine, a newly built pier made it more important than Killeany. A courthouse, a police barracks and a coastguard station were built there, giving it a completely different character from the other Inishmore clusters.

THE TRADITIONAL HOUSES OF ARAN

The traditional house type in the nineteenth-century clacháns was a long, low, single-storey cottage with a thatched roof. Though the size of these houses varied from one to three rooms, they all shared the same basic

Where the shore meets the land at Inisheer, pictured in the late nineteenth century.

design. They were rectangular structures with thick stone walls built in the dry-stone technique. Windows and doors were set in the long side of the house rather than in the gables. The roof was steeply pitched and its weight borne by the walls. All had an open hearth at floor level, with a chimney protruding through the roof ridge. The walls were usually painted with whitewash, which was reapplied every year. The roof was thatched with rye straw secured by ropes and pegs.

There were other house types to be found on the islands, such as the two-storey, slate-roofed houses that can be seen in Kilronan and some of the other larger settlements. The traditional house, however, was well adapted to climatic conditions and had the added advantage of using locally sourced materials. Windows were small and set deeply in the walls. Some cottages had no windows at all, as rent was often calculated on the basis of the size and number of windows. In any case the combination of thick stone walls, thatched roof, and small windows with even smaller panes of glass kept the house warm in winter and pleasantly cool in summer.

Doors were set in the front and back of the house, opposite each other. One or other almost always remained open by day as a means of ventilating the house and a sign of welcome to callers. The direction of the wind decided which door was opened; the open door was called the 'sheltered' door, while the closed door was called the 'wind' door.

An abandoned stone house on Aran.

There are many traditional beliefs regarding the back door, some of which are still respected. For example, it is considered unlucky for a stranger to leave the house by the back door, and when a death has occurred in the house, it is customary to carry the coffin out through the back door.

Another type of door, found both on Aran and the mainland, was the half-door. It is divided in two horizontally, allowing the lower half to remain shut while the top half can be opened for light and air. The half-door arrangement was useful for keeping young children indoors as well as preventing farm animals and hens from entering the house. It also provided a comfortable armrest for the woman or man of the house when they leaned out to chat with neighbours.

BUILDING A HOUSE

When a young man married, he would often leave the family home and build his own house with the help of friends and neighbours. The

A traditional thatched cottage.

site for the house was carefully chosen, taking account of slope, shelter and distance from other dwellings. The work of building the house was carried on in a cheerful atmosphere, and when it was completed, the owner invited his helpers and neighbours to a house-warming *céilí* (pr: kay-lee), an occasion for great celebration.

THATCHING

When the building was finished and the roof rafters had been positioned, the thatcher was called in. The thatcher was a respected craftsman who was much in demand in spring, summer and autumn. To keep the roof fully waterproofed, the thatch had to be repaired every year and the whole thatch completely renewed after seven or eight years.

Traditional Aran houses have a gable roof, which means that high gable walls rise up to the roof ridge. This arrangement is ideal for windy coastal areas. Elsewhere in Ireland, traditional houses have a four-sided or 'hip' roof, where the thatch slopes down at the sides to meet the gable at the same height as it meets the front wall.

Thatching was a reasonably cheap way of roofing a house, since the materials used were available locally. It provided a warm, dry roof in winter, and when secured properly with ropes and weights, it could withstand the fierce Atlantic gales.

It had to be repaired and renewed frequently, however, and there was always the risk that a stray spark might set the whole roof on fire. There were other challenges too: Tomás Ó Crohan, living in similar conditions on the Blasket Islands, described the problems with thatch in his book *The Islandman*:

The thatch would have been all right if the hens would only have let it alone, but they wouldn't. As soon as the rushes began to decay, and worms could be found in them, a man with a gun couldn't have kept the hens away from scratching and nesting there. Then the drips would begin, and a dirty drip it was too, for there was too much soot mixed with it.

'Thatcher'
By Seamus Heaney

Bespoke for weeks, he turned up some morning
Unexpectedly, his bicycle slung
With a light ladder and a bag of knives.
He eyed the old rigging, poked at the eaves.

Opened and handled sheaves of lashed wheat-straw.
Next, the bundled rods: hazel and willow
Were flicked for weight, twisted in case they'd snap.
It seemed he spent the morning warming up:

Then fixed the ladder, laid out well-honed blades
And snipped at straw and sharpened ends of rods
That, bent in two, made a white-pronged staple
For pinning down his world, handful by handful.

Couchant for days on sods above the rafters
He shaved and flushed the butts, stitched all together
Into a sloped honeycomb, a stubble patch,
And left them gaping at his Midas touch.

TURF

Though the Aran Islands experience heavy rainfall, surface water drains off quickly and percolates down through the many cracks in the limestone pavements that form the ground. Peat has never had the opportunity to form on this dry surface; in times past, the islanders were handicapped by the absence of bogs from which they could cut and save their own fuel. All turf used on the islands had to be purchased, and traditional wooden boats called hookers crossed from the Connemara mainland loaded with fuel. As many as fifteen boats might arrive in any one day, and the islanders would unload the turf and pay for it, usually in cash but sometimes by bartering a calf or bullock with the suppliers.

A typically small house on Aran. In the foreground, we see sheep's wool drying, having been washed and carded.

FURNITURE

The houses of Aran were small, and some structures basically consisted of a single room. Space was precious and the furniture strictly functional – chairs, a table, a dresser, beds, a wooden chest for storage and a long bench-seat which stood against the back wall. Tomás Ó Crohan describes similar furnishings on the Blaskets:

> We had bowls and plates in every house, wooden mugs, a chair or two, and a few stools. The chairs had seats of twisted rope made of hay or straw. There was a pot-rack of iron in every house, and still is, to hang things on over the fire, and there was a pair of tongs of some sort or other on the hearth.
>
> The sleeping area was not usually large enough for the whole family, so some members would sleep in the kitchen on a settle bed – a simple bedstead of wood which could be doubled up to form a high-backed bench by day. In other instances, a family might keep a bed upright against a kitchen wall and tip it down when it was needed at night.

LIGHTING

Candles and oil lamps, bought on the mainland, provided the light for houses at night. Sometimes the oil from sharks, seals or fish such as pollock was used in homemade oil lamps.

FOOD AND DRINK

Potatoes were the essential food on Aran, as elsewhere in Ireland. They were eaten in quantity for 'dinner', the main meal, which was taken at midday. They were boiled in their jackets in a large, round-bottomed iron

pot suspended from a hook over the fire. When the cooking was complete, the potatoes were removed and transferred to a plate, or sometimes a wicker basket, and placed at the side of the fire. They were seasoned with salt and butter, and milk was usually consumed with them. Other foods such as salted fish might be cooked with the potatoes.

Fresh meat was usually eaten only when a farmer killed one of his pigs or sheep. On such occasions, he would share the meat with neighbouring families; they in turn shared when they slaughtered their own animals. Bacon was home-cured and was the most frequently eaten meat. At certain festival times, families might have a chicken or goose.

A limited variety of vegetables were grown for home consumption. Families might grow onions and cabbage in a small garden near the dwelling house. Cabbage was the most popular and was frequently eaten with boiled bacon. It could also be mixed with potatoes and onions in a dish called colcannon. (This dish is more correctly made with kale, but cabbage was often used.) A plain gold ring, a sixpence, and a thimble or button were sometimes put into the colcannon dish: if you got the ring, it meant you'd be married within the year; the sixpence denoted wealth; the thimble a spinster and the button a bachelor.

White and brown wheaten flour and yellow maize flour were brought in from the mainland. Bread dough was mixed using skimmed milk and bread soda, and the bread was baked in a pot oven. This oven was a straight-sided, flat-bottomed iron pot which sat on the embers at the side of the fire. The dough was placed in the pot and the iron lid covered with glowing turf. Thus the dough was heated from both top and bottom and was baked slowly and evenly. The pot oven was also used for roasting meat or fish.

Milk and tea were drunk in every home. Buttermilk, left over from churning the butter, was considered a refreshing drink. Water for tea was boiled in a black kettle suspended from the fire crane. It was customary to keep the kettle 'on the boil' even between meals, so that tea could be brewed for anyone who called.

CLOTHES

The clothing of the Aran islanders remained traditional up to the mid-twentieth century. Men wore trousers and waistcoats of homespun tweed, grey or light brown in colour, and a brightly coloured belt called a *crios* (pr: krish) was often tied around the waist. Under the waistcoat they had a woollen sweater or *geansaí* (pr: gan-zee), which might be a natural off-white colour or sometimes dyed dark blue. Knitted socks and handmade cowhide 'slippers' or soft shoes called pampooties were the usual footwear. The Aran man also wore a knitted cap, seldom removed except in church or at mealtimes.

Women normally wore a calf-length red or dark-coloured hand-woven skirt and knitted sweater, and they wore headscarves or brightly coloured shawls when going outdoors. Like the men, they wore pampooties with black woollen socks.

Boys and girls wore long, dark-coloured petticoats of wool, even when they started school; the hem was lowered as they grew. Later they wore a scaled-down version of adult clothing. They went barefoot in summer.

SPINNING AND WEAVING

Wool was the main material used to make the locals' clothing. The sheep on the island supplied the wool, which was spun by women in the home and then sent to the local weaver, who produced the cloth on a hand loom. From this, the clothing was usually made by the local women or by a travelling tailor who lived with each family while completing their order.

In the following passage, a visitor talks to an island woman who is engaged in spinning wool for her family's clothing:

A spinning wheel used in island homes to make woollen yarn and knitting wool.

Passing the open door of a cottage one afternoon and catching a glimpse of a spinning wheel turning merrily, I paused for a moment to watch. The woman of the house, looking up, saw me and invited me in.

I felt as if I had slipped right into the middle of an old story as I sat down on a low stool by the fire. The spinning wheel, mounted on a low stand, dominated the small kitchen, and on the floor beside it was a heap of fleecy wool in soft, loose strands.

Taking a strand of wool, the woman held it beside the end of spun wool on the bobbin, then with her other hand she began turning the wheel.

'Whirr', away it went, and 'birr' sang the shuttle merrily, while in and out she pulled the thread like elastic, bent down for another strand, and 'whirr' it went again.

''Tis in a hurry I am,' she told me, 'to get it spun the way the weaver can be making a bit of flannel for me.' ...

When the bobbin was full, she brought over a ball of wool fit for a giantess to knit with, nearly seven pounds she said it weighed. It filled her whole wide red petticoat lap as she sat down and wound on the newly spun thread, while a little girl held the bobbin.

When spun it looked a dirty greyish colour, but when washed she told me it comes up 'white as the waves and them breaking'.

Then she showed me another gigantic ball, this time of dark brown wool, the natural colour of the fleece from the dark sheep.

'Them two together makes a nice bit of cloth; wait a minute now and I'll show you a bit.'

She brought over one of the sleeveless coats which the Aran men wear over their knitted jerseys. It was navy blue at the back, and this brown and white tweed in the front.

'It is how the women are the tailors on this island,' she said. 'We make everything, even the trousers.'

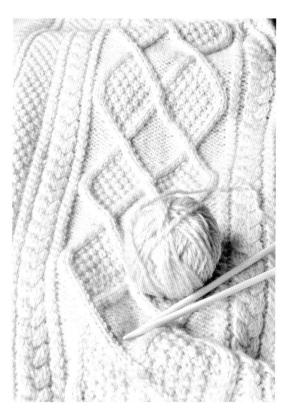

KNITTING

The women of the islands have been knitting their families' sweaters and socks for centuries. The knitting of the 'Aran jumper', with its intricate patterns of stitching, was introduced after the Famine as a means of creating employment. These sculptured, ornate sweaters quickly became part of the standard clothing of the islanders, and each family acquired its own distinctive combination of stitches. The patterns of the sweaters and socks have been used to identify bodies recovered from the sea.

The Aran knitters were remarkably proficient at this style of knitting and, working from memory, could rapidly create lines of stitching in a myriad of changing sequences of patterns.

THE CRIOS

Weaving these brightly coloured tie-belts was another distinctive craft practised by the islanders, both men and women. The weaver made a skein from lengths of different coloured wool. Then they held the skein taught by looping one end around the neck and passing a foot through the other. The hand with the wool was passed shuttle-like in and out through the strands, weaving the coloured wools through and creating a variety of radiant designs. When the weaving of the crios was finished, the strands of wool at either end were plaited into long tassles. The wearer wound the crios several times around the waist and knotted the ends together.

Aran Island women traditionally wore a calf-length, hand-woven skirt and knitted sweater, and donned a headscarf or brightly coloured shawl when going outdoors.

A group of Kilronan fishermen, near the harbour, dressed in traditional bawneens and pampooties.

PAMPOOTIES

Pampooties were the light, cow-skin shoes of the Aran islanders. The cowhide was cleaned and hung on the kitchen wall or on the rafters until required. J.M. Synge was given a pair of these shoes by the family he lodged with, and he had to learn how to walk in them. Here is his account of the incident:

> Michael walks so fast when I am out with him that I cannot pick up my steps, and the sharp-edged fossils which abound in the limestone have cut my shoes to pieces.
>
> The family held a consultation on them last night, and in the end

it was decided to make me a pair of pampooties, which I have been wearing today among the rocks.

They consist simply of a piece of raw cow-skin, with the hair outside, laced over the toe and round the heel with two ends of fishing-line that work round and are tied above the instep.

In the evening, when they are taken off, they are placed in a basin of water, as the rough hide cuts the foot and stocking if it is allowed to harden. For the same reason the people often step into the surf during the day, so that their feet are continually moist.

At first I threw my weight upon my heels, as one does naturally in a boot, and was a good deal bruised, but after a few hours I learned the natural walk of man, and could follow my guide in any portion of the island.

In one district below the cliffs, towards the north, one goes for nearly a mile jumping from one rock to another without a single ordinary step and here I realised that toes have a natural use, for I found myself jumping towards any tiny crevice in the rock before me, and clinging with an eager grip in which all the muscles of my feet ached from their exertion.

BASKET-MAKING

Basket-making was an important craft for islanders. Panniers for the donkey's back, storage baskets for turf and potatoes, dish-baskets for cooked potatoes, 'spillet' baskets for the fishermen's long lines – all were made from the willow shoots, known locally as 'sally' rods, which grow in little groves around the island.

In traditional basket-making, uprights are planted in the ground and a 'wall' is created by weaving lighter willow rods in and out between them.

Cows were seldom housed in a byre on Aran but left in the fields in both summer and winter. Goats were traditionally kept by many families, providing milk and hides.

CHAPTER THREE

FARMING AND FISHING

THE ARAN FARMERS

Today the main industries on Aran are fishing and, increasingly, tourism. In days gone by, when the islands were practically self-sufficient, fishing was also important, as were kelp-making, spinning, weaving and basket-making, while small-scale farming was the primary industry of many an Aran family.

Each clachán housed a number of families who held the surrounding land in common ownership. A fence enclosed a large tract of arable land, known as the infield, where each farmer had strips to grow crops. The unfenced pasture, or rough grazing, owned by the group was called the outfield, and each farmer was entitled to graze their animals there. The land was fairly evenly divided among the farmers, with each holding consisting of between seventeen and twenty acres. Most farmers also owned a portion of the sea-shore, where they could gather seaweed for fertiliser; some good fields, suitable for growing potatoes and grazing cattle; some rough grazing for sheep; and also some of the almost useless

bare-stone flagging. This meant, of course, that a family's fields might be widely scattered, and such a farm was described as 'fragmented'.

The pattern of work moved up and down the slope with the seasons. Downslope of the houses were the patches of arable land and pasture, while upslope on the hilltops and the crags were the winter pastures. Carrying water to the livestock in summer was an easy downhill journey performed by the women, while the men were busily engaged in fishing. The more difficult uphill journey in winter was regarded as a man's job.

Rye was the only grain crop grown on Aran. As on the mainland, potatoes were the staple diet. Due to the poor quality of the soil, they had to be sown by hand in furrowed lazybeds. The islanders were not tolerant of those who did not pull their weight. A farmer who did not sow his potatoes on time was contemptuously referred to as a 'cuckoo farmer', because he was still seeding his crop when the first call of the cuckoo was heard in April.

Farming on Aran required ingenuity, dedication and back-breaking work. Firstly the farmer had to create fields in which to grow crops by choosing an area of flat rock in a suitable location. He would even the surface by knocking off any outcrops of rock – although the ground could not be completely smooth or the soil spread on it would be blown away. Large gaps were filled up with pieces of rock to prevent the soil from trickling down through them. The surface was then covered with layers of sand that had been carted up from the beach. Finally, a layer of precious soil was laid on top. This soil was gathered from the crevices between the rocks and from the more fertile parts of the island. But fertiliser was also required, and the only ones available to the Aran farmer who wished to improve his stony fields were sand and seaweed. The sand found on Aran's beaches was created by the erosion of limestone rock, which meant it was highly calcareous and therefore suitable for growing potatoes. Certain kinds of seaweed served the same function and were hauled to the fields at seeding time using a donkey and panniers.

This laborious method of preparing the land for crops ensured that fields were kept very small, resulting in the maze-like field patterns, hemmed in by a patchwork of stone walls, which we see on Aran today. Each little field was surrounded by a stone wall. The walls were quite high

and a convenient place for the farmer to put rocks and boulders cleared from his land. Stones were carefully selected and positioned so that the wind could pass freely through the gaps between them. In this way, they could withstand the fierce force of the south-westerly gales. Even today, when the wind passes through the walls it often makes an eerie whistling sound over the islands, like a forlorn banshee. The walls are modern examples of the dry-stone masonry found in the ancient forts; neither mortar nor cement was used.

Metal and timber had to be imported from the mainland and so were in short supply on the islands. Therefore 'gates' in the walls were also made of rocks. When a wall was being built, an entrance gap several metres wide was left open. When the wall was completed, the gap was filled in with rounded stones. Each time a farmer wished to drive his cattle into the field, he knocked down this 'gate'. The rounded stones tumbled down quite easily and could be rebuilt afterwards without much trouble.

Cattle were highly valued by the Aran Islands farmers. The size of a farm was seldom described in acres; instead, someone might have been said to have *féar dhá bhó* (pr: fare gaw voh; 'the grass of two cows'). Cattle were grazed on scattered patches of grassland, which were cordoned off for the purpose. As in the Burren, the winters here are relatively mild, and – unlike in other parts of Ireland – cattle were left out in the fields all year round. During a severe winter, when there was not enough grass to graze on, the farmer would carry bundles of rye to the fields for the cows. When nothing else was available, he might even feed them a mixture of bran and potatoes. Other animals kept by Aran farmers included horses, pigs, sheep, goats and donkeys. All had to be sturdy to survive on the islands.

A typical pattern of maze-like fields, hemmed in by a patchwork of stone walls.

FISHING

To this day, the men of Aran are skilful and competent fishermen. The abundance of fish has been essential to the islanders' survival since monastic times. The sea allowed them to supplement the meagre living afforded by their rocky fields; it protected them in times of invasion, and in the hungry famine years, it gave them the food that saved them from starvation. But the sea is also cruel. It isolated the islanders, battered them with violent storms and cut them off over long periods from out-side human contact and medical aid. Time and again, it claimed the lives of the islandmen.

The islands' fishermen respect the sea, knowing the dangers of its ever-changing moods. Very few of them can swim, however. They like to say that if you cannot swim, you'll be more careful on the sea, and that for

The wreck of the freighter *Plassey*, which ran ashore on the eastern edge of Inisheer in 1960.

Above: Boats in Kilronan Harbour, Inishmore.

Below: Traditional curraghs are used for annual inter-island races.

the non-swimmer, death by drowning will be quicker without a struggle.

The tradition and legend of the Aran jumper or geansaí grew up around fishing: each family had its own particular pattern, so that when a fisherman was washed up, he could be identified by his geansaí. This story is poignant and assumed to be ancient, but the Aran jumper is largely a twentieth-century invention – though perhaps invented precisely for this purpose, who knows? In his famous Aran play *Riders to the Sea*, first performed in 1904, J.M. Synge describes the sad event of Cathleen and Nora having to identify their brother Michael, lost at sea, by his clothing, especially the knitting:

(Cathleen opens the bundle and takes out a bit of a shirt and a stocking. They look at them eagerly.)

CATHLEEN *(in a low voice)*: The Lord spare us, Nora! Isn't it a queer hard thing to say if it's his they are surely?

NORA: I'll get his shirt off the hook the way we can put the one flannel on the other. *(She looks through some clothes hanging in the corner.)* It's not with them, Cathleen, and where will it be?

CATHLEEN: I'm thinking Bartley put it on him in the morning, for his own shirt was heavy with the salt in it. *(Pointing to the corner.)* There's a bit of a sleeve was of the same stuff. Give me that and it will do. *(Nora brings it to her and they compare the flannel.)*

CATHLEEN: It's the same stuff, Nora; but if it is itself, aren't there great rolls of it in the shops of Galway, and isn't it many another man may have a shirt of it as well as Michael himself?

NORA *(who has taken up the stocking and counted the stitches, crying out)*: It's Michael, Cathleen, it's Michael; God spare his soul, and what will herself say when she hears this story, and Bartley on the sea?

CATHLEEN *(taking the stocking)*: It's a plain stocking.

NORA: It's the second one of the third pair I knitted, and I put up three-score stitches, and I dropped four of them.

CATHLEEN *(counts the stitches)*: It's that number is in it. (*Crying out.*) Ah Nora, isn't it a bitter thing to think of him floating that way to the far north, and no one to keen him but the black hags that do be flying on the sea?

NORA *(swinging herself half round, and throwing out her arms on the clothes)*: And isn't it a pitiful thing when there is nothing left of a man who was a great rower and fisher but a bit of an old shirt and a plain stocking?

The islanders engaged in different types of fishing, employing different types of gear, all handmade. The clean vertical face of the cliffs, free of any rock outcrops, allowed the men to engage in cliff-fishing with a heavily weighted hand-line. This practice was commonly used for fishing wrasse, known locally as rockfish, and mackerel, pollock and bass.

In the mid-nineteenth century, a tragedy occurred at Glassan Rock (*Aill na nGlasóg*) near the southeastern end of Inishmore, which is still recalled on the island today. Fifteen men from Killeany were fishing from a cliff ledge when they were swept into the sea by a freak wave and drowned. Almost every household in the little village was bereaved of a husband or son in the disaster, which, according to popular lore, was occasioned by the fact that the men had not attended Mass on the day in question, which was a holy day. Such disasters remain in the collective memory of the islands for a long, long time, and are still discussed

as if they happened recently.

The boat used for sea-fishing was the age-old currach (also spelled *curach* or *curragh*), an open canoe ideally suited to conditions around the Aran Islands. Drift nets were used to catch mackerel and herring. The nets, which floated in an upright position near the surface, were laid at night when they were invisible to the fish. The catch was hauled in first thing in the morning. The Aran writer Thomas O'Flaherty tells how the currach was launched:

I, being the tallest of the four, crawled under the curach, got my shoulders under the first stand. Two men, one on each side of the prow, lifted the boat with me. When I was straight, holding up the prow, another man got under the rear seat and straightened up. A third shouldered a middle seat, and then this boat, that has been likened when carried in this fashion to a 'gigantic beetle on stilts', was walked to the water. A fourth member of the crew followed with the oars on his shoulder. Our curach was the first to be laid on the strand ready for launching. We turned her prow to the surf and put the eight oars on the pins. Several men who had not yet decided to go to sea gathered around our curach. We pushed her out until she was afloat. Then the four of us took our seats. We held our oars poised over the water, ready to start rowing at a signal from the look-out man. Six men held the curach straight in the face of the waves while we waited for a lull. Then the look-out shouted hoarsely: 'Stick her out! Give her the oars!'

The six men dug their pampootie-clad feet into the sand and pushed the curach quickly towards the sea. Our eight oars struck the water simultaneously. We seemed to be rowing in a pond for a moment, the sea was so smooth. Then the curach rose sharply and almost stood on end, straight as an arrow in a big sea. Down she came on the other side with a crash that set the teeth shaking in our mouths.

As the first sea fell on the strand we rose on another, not as dangerous as the first because we were in deeper water, but bad enough to prove our undoing if the curach's head was turned an inch too far to the right or left.

We rowed, putting our oars far forward and bringing them to a feather with a graceful flourish. My uncle sang joyously in a voice that was everything but melodious. We were now out of danger, in the long lazy swell of the deep water.

As we rowed towards our nets, we could see the prow of another curach rising over the crest of the sea, then disappearing in the trough. Then another curach got safely through the gauntlet of shore breakers.

Sea-rods, which are the stalks of seaweed, being stacked. They were exported for chemical processing; one of the main extracts was iodine.

Long-lines were used to catch those fish which live on or near the seabed, including 'round' fish like cod, ling and pollock, and 'flat' fish like plaice, sole and turbot. The long lines, as the name suggests, were about two- to three hundred metres in length and had a hundred or more hooks attached. The hooks were baited with slugs or salt fish and the long-line was anchored in a suitable location and left overnight. Two buoys at either end marked its position.

Lobsters and cray fish required a different method of trapping. Lobster pots made from willow or thin laths were weighted with stones. Several pots were attached to a rope and lowered into the water, their position marked by a buoy. The bait in the pot coaxed the lobster or cray fish inside. Once they entered, the door shut behind them and they were trapped, ready for collection.

The work of the fishermen was difficult and dangerous. Although suited to the task, currachs were still prey for rogue waves and high seas.

Kelp-making

Kelp-making was an important and profitable enterprise for the islanders in the nineteenth and early twentieth centuries. Kelp is an iodine-rich substance produced by burning red seaweed. The islanders sold this substance to factories on the mainland, where it was used in the making of chemicals, soap and glass. The red seaweed grows underwater and was best gathered after the autumn and winter storms. Often the islanders had to wade thigh-deep in the icy water to cut the seaweed from submerged rocks. The work had to be done on a calm day when the tides were low. Knives and sickles attached to long handles were used for cutting the weed in deeper water. This deep-water weed was prized, as it was entirely free of sand.

In his book *Cliffmen of the West* (1935), Thomas O'Flaherty talks about the best seaweed for kelp-making:

Every year about the first of May the Big Breaker half way between Aran and Conamara rears its crest and sends mighty waves speeding towards the shore. All along the bayside of the island lesser breakers come in its wake, and the red seaweed that grows in the shallow places is torn up by the roots and carried to land by the currents. The best kelp is made from this red weed if it gets to the shore quickly, and is spread out to dry before it loses some of the precious juice in deep sea holes and in the burrows under the rocks. Seaweed that is washed ashore on a sandy beach is almost useless for kelp-making.

To the shores of boulders and pebbles the men take their straddled horses, a basket on each side with ropes made of horsehair attached. High over the straddle they pile the seaweed and hold it together

with the ropes. And those hard Aran ponies of the Conamara strain pick their way over slippery, moss-covered flags, between large boulders and pebbles that give way under pressure of hoof, with the sureness of goats among the crags of a mountain.

The seaweed was carried up from the shore in panniers by donkey or horse. It was hard, heavy work as it took more than twenty-five tonnes of seaweed to make one tonne of kelp, and the work had to be completed quickly while tides were favourable. If a family did not own a donkey, they had to carry the weed in baskets on their backs. Because the men were busy cutting the weed, women sometimes did the carrying work,

wearing an animal hide on their backs as protection.

When gathered, the seaweed was laid out to dry on walls and rocks. Then it was piled up in ricks, not unlike haycocks, where it was left until early June, the usual time for making kelp. A kelp kiln – a low, rectangular stone trough capable of holding about two tonnes of seaweed – was constructed for burning the dried-out seaweed. Firing had to be done properly as the kelp would be ruined if not given enough time to 'run', or if fired for too long. As the weed began to melt, it was stirred with long iron rakes until it turned into a molten mass. When the firing was complete, the kelp was left in the kiln to cool. After a few days it was as hard as limestone and had to be broken up with a sledge-hammer before being transported in currachs to Kilronan. There, it was tested for quality and the kelp-burner received due payment. Later, the steamer took it to the mainland.

'The Oarsmen's Song'
By Seamus Heaney

It's only twice a week she comes
How we look forward to that day.
Like some good omen to our homes
She blows her note across the bay.
There's bread in chests and oil in drums,
A wardrobe and a mattress
A box of nibs, a card of combs,
And a mail bag full of letters.

As black and hollow as huge pods,
The currachs dandle on the wave,
Wild winch and pulley lower the goods,
The sailors shout, the seagulls rave.
There's whitewash brushes, bags of nails,
With bottled gas and liquor,
Long iron gates, enamel pails,
And a hamper made of wicker.

What we can't load we float behind –
Slim planks for rafters, boards for floors,
Back from the steamer to the land
We're lying heavy on the oars:
With tins of polish, panes of glass,
And shafts for scythes and shafts for spades,
A pram, a cot, a plastic bath,
And shaving soap and razor blades.

ANGLIAE, SCOTIAE, ET HIBERNIAE, SIVE BRITANNICAR: INSVLARVM DESCRIPTIO.

CHAPTER FOUR

A Brief History of Aran

Although the islands are remote and their people for many centuries lived a self-contained life, the Aran Islands also played a part in the general history of Ireland. The Normans first arrived in Ireland at the behest of Dermot MacMurrough, King of Leinster. He had been deprived of his territory after he quarrelled with the High King and another Irish chieftain, O'Rourke of Breifne, so he fled to England, where he recruited a band of Norman knights and foot soldiers. With this force, he returned to Ireland in 1169 and rapidly conquered the fertile lands around the old Viking towns of Waterford, Wexford and Dublin. Dermot died, leaving the Norman knights in possession of large tracts of land. King Henry II, the overlord of the Normans, was crowned King of Ireland.

The Norman settlers initially confined themselves largely to the east of the country, and it was not until the fourteenth century that they attempted to subdue the wild and isolated west coast. The Lord Justice,

Opposite: An antique map of Britain by Abraham Ortelius, circa 1570.

King Henry II of England, who was also crowned King of Ireland.

one of the king's deputies, sailed up the west coast in 1334. Contemporary records show that he plundered Inishmore, which, along with Inisheer, had a considerable population at this time. It is thought that Inishmaan was uninhabited, except for a few hermits.

The O'Briens, who controlled much of what are now counties Clare and Limerick, were allowed to continue as lords of the islands because the walled city of Galway had come to depend on their goodwill as masters

O'Brien's Castle on Inisheer.

of Galway Bay: they accepted an annual payment from the citizens for controlling piracy and as a guarantee against interference with trade to and from the city. This arrangement suited both parties, and they tolerated each other in peace. On Aran, the O'Briens built a fortified tower house – O'Brien's Castle (*Caisleán Uí Bhriain*) – within the walls of Dún Formna. They may also have built a small castle at Killeany, and they were the patrons of the Franciscan monastery established there in 1480.

The mainland of Ireland was less peaceful than the islands during the fourteenth, fifteenth and sixteenth centuries, as the Norman English gradually increased their influence. Certain branches of the Gaelic clans were prepared to recognise the English king as their ruler in order to gain control of the clan lands with his support. Such a conflict developed in 1584 among the O'Flahertys of west Galway, which resulted in the clan chief and his followers fleeing to Aran, where they found refuge with the O'Briens. The victorious branch of the clan, who had been supported by the English, pursued the fugitives and finally defeated them and their allies, the O'Briens; the Aran Islands then passed into the hands of the O'Flahertys. The reign of the O'Briens was at an end, though they would make repeated efforts to regain their lost lands.

The O'Briens appealed to the Crown, and a commission was established in Galway City in 1587 to decide on the ownership of the islands. The government, however, decided to annex the islands, which they saw as being of strategic importance in the defence of the kingdom against the French and Spanish. The decision was made on the grounds that the islands were monastery land and that, as the monasteries of Ireland and England had been suppressed by law and their lands taken over by the Crown, the islands were the rightful property of the queen. In the

The sheltered harbour of Killeany on Inishmore, once home to Arkyne's Castle, a fort that played a pivotal role in the history of Ireland.

government's view, neither the O'Briens nor the O'Flahertys could be trusted, and so the islands were granted to John Rawson of Athlone on condition that he keep a garrison of soldiers there. Thus the ownership of the land of Aran passed from those who lived on it and worked it.

John Rawson – believed to have been the builder of Arkyne's Castle (*Caisleán Aircín*), located overlooking Killeany harbour – sold the islands to the Lynch family of Galway in 1588. The fort was to play a pivotal role in the conquest of the island.

Seventeenth-century Ireland was ravaged by almost continuous warfare. By the middle of the century, the battle lines were being drawn on a new basis: religion. In 1642, some native Irish chiefs and Anglo-Norman lords united in the Confederation of Kilkenny, the aim of which was the restoration of the Catholic religion. Their opponent, Oliver Cromwell, the Lord Protector of England, landed in Dublin in 1649. He waged total war on his enemies, capturing the major towns and laying waste to the countryside. Tens of thousands of civilians were given the option 'to Hell or Connacht', and were driven westward by his victorious army. The fertile lands that they had been forced to vacate were given to planters from England and Scotland. It seems probable that some of the dispossessed who were forced to cross the River Shannon into Connacht may have settled on the islands at this time.

Oliver Cromwell.

The Marquis of Clanricarde, one of the leaders on the Irish side, hoped that the tide could be turned if his French allies sent troops to Ireland as promised. He garrisoned the Aran Islands in order to preserve a point of entry for this anticipated arrival. Sir Robert Lynch, the owner of the islands, was given the title of Commander-in-Chief and supplied with two hundred soldiers. Arkyne's Castle was fortified, and Inishmore was placed on a war footing. The French force failed to arrive, and the Irish were repeatedly defeated. Galway City fell to the Cromwellians in December 1650, though seven hundred officers and men from its garrison escaped to Inishbofin.

The small Aran garrison surrendered, and a body of Cromwell's troops was sent to hold the island and strengthen Arkyne's Castle. They demolished a number of ancient churches at St Enda's monastery and used the stone as building material. While they were engaged in this work (in 1652), the Irish troops from Inishbofin took them by surprise and regained control of Arkyne. A Cromwellian force of 1,300 men, under the command of General Reynolds, laid siege to the fort. The Irish garrison surrendered within a week and was allowed to take ship for the Continent. Sir Robert Lynch was declared a traitor and his lands forfeit. The islands became the property of a Cromwellian, Erasmus Smith. This explains why the fort is known to the locals as Ballaí Chromwell, or Cromwell's Walls.

During the next decade, the government strengthened the defences of Arkyne's Castle and made use of it as a prison camp for Catholic priests awaiting deportation to the West Indies. (During the Reformation, all Roman Catholic priests were automatically deemed guilty of high treason.) A garrison was maintained on the islands, but in the more peaceful era of the eighteenth century, the fortifications of Arkyne's Castle were allowed to crumble and the number of men stationed there dwindled. In the meantime, the islands changed hands on several occasions. Erasmus Smith sold his interest to the Butlers of Ormonde. Richard Butler received the title Earl of Arran in 1662 but this family soon parted with the land, and those who later held the title had no connection with Aran. The garrison finally departed in 1685.

During the eighteenth and nineteenth centuries, the islands were owned by a succession of absentee landlords whose sole interest was in the income they received from rents. The Fitzmaurices of Galway City owned the islands for a time but lost them to the Digby family of County Kildare early in the nineteenth century, on a mortgage that they failed to repay. In 1870, Elizabeth Digby married and became Countess of Howth, and the ownership of Aran passed to her two surviving daughters. Agents who were placed in charge extracted huge rents from the island tenants, whose living conditions worsened rapidly.

A small field on Inishmaan.

LAND OWNERSHIP

From the eighteenth century on, pressure on the land became more severe with each succeeding generation. The rule of primogeniture, in which the first-born inherits the farm, had never been observed in Ireland. Instead, a farmer divided his land between all of his surviving children, and so, within a generation or two, quite large farms were reduced to a collection of individually owned patches. The tenants who farmed such patches on Aran were rack-rented by their landlords, who often collected £2,000 per annum. Contributing their share to this huge rent was often too great a burden on the tenants, who would fall into arrears. When this occurred, there was no mercy for the tenant farmers, and evictions were common. J.M. Synge witnessed and described the eviction of several Inishmaan farmers for non-payment of rent:

Two recent attempts to carry out evictions on the island came to nothing, for each time a sudden storm rose, by, it is said, the power of a native witch, when the steamer was approaching, and made it impossible to land.

This morning, however, broke beneath a clear sky of June and when I came into the open air the sea and rocks were shining with wonderful brilliancy. Groups of men, dressed in their holiday clothes, were standing about, talking with anger and fear, yet showing a lurking satisfaction at the thought of the dramatic pageant that was to break the silence of the seas.

About half-past nine the steamer came in sight on the narrow line of sea-horizon that is seen in the centre of the bay, and immediately a last effort was made to hide the cows and sheep of the families that were most in debt.

Till this year no one on the island would consent to act as bailiff, so that it was impossible to identify the cattle of the defaulters. Now, however, a man of the name of Patrick has sold his honour, and the effort of concealment is practically futile.

This falling away from the ancient loyalty of the island has caused intense indignation and early yesterday morning, while I was dreaming on the Dun, this letter was nailed on the doorpost of the chapel:

Patrick, the devil, a revolver is waiting for you. If you are missed with the first shot, there will be five more that will hit you. Any man that will talk with you, or work with you, or drink a pint of porter in your shop, will be done with the same way as yourself.

As the steamer drew near I moved down with the men to watch the arrival, though no one went further than about a mile from the

Across the waters in Moyasta, County Clare, in the 1880s, police use a battering ram to evict tentants unable to pay their rent.

shore. Two curaghs from Kilronan with a man who was to give help in identifying the cottages, the doctor, and the relieving officer, were drifting with the tide, unwilling to come to land without the support of the larger party. When the anchor had been thrown it gave me a strange throb of pain to see the boats being lowered, and the sunshine gleaming on the rifles and helmets of the constabulary who crowded into them.

Once on shore the men were formed in close marching order, a word was given, and the heavy rhythm of their boots came up over the rocks. We were collected in two straggling bands on either side of the roadway, and a few moments later the body of magnificent armed men passed close to us, followed by a low rabble, who had been brought to act as drivers for the sheriff.

After my weeks spent among primitive men this glimpse of the newer types of humanity was not reassuring. Yet these mechanical police, with the commonplace agents and sheriffs, and the rabble they had hired, represented aptly enough the civilization for which the homes of the island were to be desecrated.

A stop was made at one of the first cottages in the village, and the day's work began. Here, however, and at the next cottage, a compromise was made, as some relatives came up at the last moment and lent the money that was needed to gain a respite.

In another case a girl was ill in the house, so the doctor interposed, and the people were allowed to remain after a merely formal eviction. About midday, however, a house was reached where there was no pretext for mercy, and no money could be procured. At a sign from the sheriff the work of carrying out the beds and utensils was begun in

the middle of a crowd of natives who looked on in absolute silence, broken only by the wild imprecations of the woman of the house. She belonged to one of the most primitive families on the island, and she shook with uncontrollable fury as she saw the strange armed men who spoke a language she could not understand driving her from the hearth she had brooded on for thirty years. For these people the outrage to the hearth is the supreme catastrophe. They live here in a world of grey, where there are wild rains and mists every week in the year, and their warm chimney corners, filled with children and young girls, grow into the consciousness of each family in a way it is not easy to understand in more civilized places.

The outrage to a tomb in China probably gives no greater shock to the Chinese than the outrage to a hearth in Inishmaan gives to the people.

When the few trifles had been carried out, and the door blocked with stones, the old woman sat down by the threshold and covered her head with her shawl.

Five or six other women who lived close by sat down in a circle round her, with mute sympathy. Then the crowd moved on with the police to another cottage where the same scene was to take place, and left the group of desolate women sitting by the hovel.

There were still no clouds in the sky, and the heat was intense. The police when not in motion lay sweating and gasping under the walls with their tunics unbuttoned. They were not attractive, and I kept comparing them with the islandmen, who walked up and down as cool and fresh-looking as the sea-gulls.

When the last eviction had been carried out a division was made: half the party went off with the bailiff to search the inner plain of the island for the cattle that had been hidden in the morning, the other half remained on the village road to guard some pigs that had already been taken possession of.

After a while two of these pigs escaped from the drivers and began a wild race up and down the narrow road. The people shrieked and howled to increase their terror, and at last some of them became so excited that the police thought it time to interfere. They drew up in double line opposite the mouth of a blind laneway where the animals had been shut up. A moment later the shrieking began again in the west and the two pigs came in sight, rushing down the middle of the road with the drivers behind them.

They reached the line of the police. There was a slight scuffle, and then the pigs continued their mad rush to the east, leaving three policemen lying in the dust.

The satisfaction of the people was immense. They shrieked and hugged each other with delight, and it is likely that they will hand down these animals for generations in the tradition of the island.

Two hours later the other party returned, driving three lean cows before them, and a start was made for the slip. At the public-house the policemen were given a drink while the dense crowd that was following waited in the lane. The island bull happened to be in a field close by, and he became wildly excited at the sight of the cows and of the strangely dressed men. Two young islanders sidled up to me in a moment or two as I was resting on a wall, and one of them whispered in my ear:

'Do you think they could take fines of us if we let out the bull on them?'

In face of the crowd of women and children, I could only say it was probable, and they slunk off.

At the slip there was a good deal of bargaining, which ended in all the cattle being given back to their owners. It was plainly of no use to take them away, as they were worth nothing.

When the last policemen had embarked, an old woman came forward from the crowd and, mounting on a rock near the slip, began a fierce rhapsody in Gaelic, pointing at the bailiff and waving her withered arms with extraordinary rage.

'This man is my own son,' she said, 'it is I that ought to know him. He is the first ruffian in the whole big world.'

Then She gave an account of his life, coloured with a vindictive fury I cannot reproduce. As she went on the excitement became so intense I thought the man would be stoned before he could get back to his cottage.

On these islands the women live only for their children, and it is hard to estimate the power of the impulse that made this old woman stand out and curse her son.

In the fury of her speech I seem to look again into the strange reticent temperament of the islanders, and to feel the passionate spirit that expresses itself, at odd moments only, with magnificent words and gestures.

This situation was intolerable for the farmers, and they joined the Land League to campaign for 'The Three Fs': Fair Rent, Fixity of Tenure and Freedom of Sale. They were granted these demands by the British parliament in Prime Minister Gladstone's Land Acts of 1881 and 1882. Under these acts, a tenant and his family could remain on their farm even if the rent were in arrears, and they also had the right to sell their interest in the farm to any other person. This led to the setting up of purchase schemes, whereby the English government made money available at low interest rates to the tenants so they could buy out their holdings.

By 1910, four million hectares of land had changed hands as a result of these schemes, but the process of reform was slow in some areas. It was not until 1922 that the landlords of Aran, the Digby-St Lawrence family, sold their interest in the islands and the Aran farmers became the owners of their own land.

Inisheer lighthouse.
Inset: The old lighthouse on Inishmore.

LIGHTHOUSES

The nineteenth century saw the first lighthouses built on Aran to aid sea-farers. The first lighthouse was built in 1818 at the highest point of Inishmore, near Dún Eochla. It is a prominent feature of the Inishmore skyline from almost any vantage point on the island. It was, however, too high to be of any use as a beacon in foggy conditions; even in clear conditions, ships lying in close to the cliffs on the south side could not see the light that might have warned them of their danger. As a result, it was decommissioned. It was soon replaced by two new structures: one at Eeragh on Rock Island (*An tOileán Íarthach*), a tiny outcrop of rock off the northeastern edge of Inishmore; the other on Inisheer. These light-houses were made from local limestone and painted with striped bands.

Both were manned until 1978, at which time they were automated. In 1878, a lighthouse was built on the eleven-acre Straw Island (*Oileán na Tuí*) to guide vessels into Kilronan harbour. It too was decommissioned, in 1926. A similar lighthouse was erected at Poinnte an Fhardarus, on the southeastern tip of Inisheer, to light the other extremity of the islands.

When manned, the lighthouses were watched over by keepers who worked one month on and one month off. We can only imagine how lonely their lives were, stranded on a rocky outcrop with only the gulls for company. It must have been a strange and solitary life, and no doubt the men looked forward to seeing their friends and families again at the end of each long month spent tending the light.

The magnificent Dún Aengus on Inishmore.

CHAPTER FIVE

THE ANCIENT FORTS
OF ARAN

For the visitor approaching the Aran Islands, the horizon is dominated by the massive outlines of the stone forts which contribute to the grandeur of the landscape. Indeed, few areas in Ireland are so rich in ancient remains – some spectacular, some less so – as are these three islands. William Wilde, the nineteenth-century antiquarian and father of the more famous Oscar, noted that 'the Western Islands of Aran contain the greatest number of pagan and Early Christian monuments – military, domestic, ecclesiastical and sepulchral – which can be found within the same area in Europe'. The islands have been home to waves of settlers for millennia, but if we look for signs of the very earliest inhabitants, we find only the most tantalising traces of their presence.

Based on the evidence for early communities of farmers in the Burren and in Connemara, archaeologists believe it is likely that the sea routes of the west of Ireland brought people here in their skin boats as early as

The remains of a dolmen on Inishmaan. This tomb is one of the indications that the islands were inhabited in the Megalithic period.

4000BC. They probably came from the European mainland, which they left in search of new lands. These new arrivals would have been the first humans to set foot on Aran's bare stones. They probably hunted and fished on the islands from that time, although there are no traces of the rough shelters they must have built. The first definite evidence for the inhabitation of Aran dates to around 2500BC and is provided by the presence of megalithic tombs, now mostly in ruins.

During what we know as the Neolithic period or the New Stone Age, these people settled and began to grow crops and tend their animals. They also built stone monuments to commemorate their dead. These are evidence that an early farming community was settled enough to build megalithic structures to honour their ancestors and to establish their claim to the land.

The type of megalithic tomb found on Aran is known as the wedge tomb, a burial monument that was in vogue around 2000BC, during the Late Neolithic period. The wedge-shaped plan to which it is built gives this tomb type its name; it resembles a large stone coffin. As these tombs are almost always oriented towards the setting sun, it seems likely that a belief in the afterlife and a connection with the power of the sun formed part of the beliefs of our Stone Age ancestors.

The remains of at least half a dozen of these wedge tombs can be found on Aran. Eight kilometres away in the Burren in County Clare, there are many more such tombs – early evidence of the close connections between the Aran Islands and the Burren. Some lie in ruins on the islands today, but on Inishmore a fine example still stands at Eochaill,

Dún Eochla on Inishmore is a well-preserved example of an oval-shaped hill fort.

O'Brien's Castle, part of Dún Formna on Inisheer.

on a ridge southwest of Teampall an Cheathrair Álainn ('the Church of the Four Beauties'). It consists of two large slabs of stone buttressed by an end-stone, with the three slabs capped by three roof slabs. Another ruined wedge tomb on Inishmore stands at Fearann A' Choirce (Oatlands), over-looking the seashore to the north. On Inishmaan two collapsed mega-lithic structures are further examples. One of these lies close to Baile an Mhothair (Moher), the other in Ceathrú an Teampaill (Carrowntemple) on the northwestern coast. There were, no doubt, many other burial sites on Aran which have not withstood the rigours of the millennia.

Tombs of this type are commonly found to contain cremated burials, pottery shards and some personal belongings, such as beads and amulets. But otherwise they keep their secrets so that we can only speculate as to the burial rituals that would have taken place here as people consigned the remains of their ancestors to the afterlife.

From around 1800BC, Bronze Age people found their way here, too. They had the advantage of having metal tools and the knowledge of how to make them. These communities buried their dead under stone cairns, placing the remains in beautifully decorated urns. Two such burial urns came to light in 1885 in a mound at Cnoc Raithní on Inisheer; they date to about 1500BC. Other Bronze Age finds have been made on Inisheer – a stone battleaxe was unearthed at Baile an Lugáin, and a bronze socketed axehead was found at Dún Formna.

The most obvious legacy of the early life of the island, however, is of course the massive stone forts which dominate the landscape and the imagination.

THE GREAT STONE FORTS

Rising up from the stones of Aran are the great forts and cashels which have come to define these islands. The most famous and most impressive of these monuments is Dun Aengus (*Dún Aonghasa*) on Inishmore, which George Petrie described as 'the most magnificent barbaric monument in Europe'. There are six other great forts: also on Inishmore are Dúcathair, a promontory fort in the southeast, and Dún Eochla and Dún Eoghanachta on inland sites; on Inishmaan are Dún Chonchúir and Dún Fhearbhaigh; and on Inisheer the fort of Dún Formna encompasses the medieval O'Brien's Castle within its walls. Three of the forts – Dun Aengus, Dúcathair and Dún Chonchúir – have their origins in prehistoric times, while the rest were probably built in the early medieval period. The forts vary considerably in size and in the complexity of their defences, some being univallate, that is, having one enclosing wall, while others are multivallate, having three or more walls.

For centuries these forts have excited the interest of antiquarians and archaeologists, and indeed all visitors to the islands. In folk tradition they had a heroic status and were perceived as the strongholds of the Fir Bolg, an early mythical race who feature in the origin legends of this country. The forts have long been considered to be pre-Christian in origin, and the presence of *chevaux-de-frise* at some sites (upright, sharp-edged pillars of stone set closely together at regular intervals as a defensive obstacle) suggests links with forts in Spain, Wales and Scotland, where *chevaux-de-frise* are also a feature. Scholars believe it possible that the forts could represent a route along which Celtic people and influences reached Ireland.

DUN AENGUS ON INISHMORE

Dun Aengus is the most imposing and splendid of the great stone forts. Situated on the northwestern coast of Inishmore, on the edge of a sheer cliff eighty-seven metres high, it is one of the most important of the many dry-stone forts scattered along the coast of Ireland, from Kerry to Donegal.

It is amazing to think that a small community of people settled on the edge of this windblown cliff around 1300BC, before a stone of Dun Aengus was laid. They might well have built a wall to act as a windbreak for their rude shelters, and that wall might have been incorporated into the fort. We cannot be sure as we have only scant information on their lives, although excavations by the Discovery Programme's Western Stone

Above and below: Dun Aengus.

The dramatic cliffs near Dun Aengus.

Forts Project, conducted between 1992 and 1995, testify to the presence of a group of people here over three millennia ago. What part they played in the building of the great fort is uncertain, but it is gradually becoming clear that the people of the Late Bronze Age were building the early phases of what we know as hill forts today.

Dun Aengus is a massive structure, all the more awe-inspiring for having been designed and built by people who, by modern standards, had only the most rudimentary tools (although their stone-working skills were far superior!). It is made of massive blocks of limestone, quarried on site. The blocks are carefully placed to withstand time and weather, despite the fact that the entire structure is dry-stone built, that is, without mortar.

The fort encloses almost 14.5 acres. It comprises a semi-circular walled enclosure, open to the sea on one side and surrounded by three further roughly concentric walls, all of which terminate at a cliff edge with a sheer drop of several hundred metres to the pounding Atlantic waves below. The innermost rampart is four metres wide at the base and rises to a height of six metres. On the eastern side is a doorway with its massive lintels still in place. This great rampart also has terraces and half a dozen sets of steps. In the centre of the enclosure, backing onto the lip of the cliff, is a rectangular platform, a natural rock outcrop, although it has been described as a man-made table, or altar.

Archaeological excavations by the Discovery Programme recovered pieces of amber, a precious commodity, which indicates that people of wealth were living and presumably trading here. The first evidence for domestic dwellings in the central enclosure dates to 800BC and consists of the foundations of circular huts and some pottery fragments. The

The *cheveaux-de-frise* of Dun Aengus. This remarkable barrier of razor-sharp standing stones was a defensive measure.

An aerial view of Dun Aengus.

most significant find for the archaeologists of the Discovery Programme were clay moulds used in the making of objects such as swords, knives, spearheads, axe-heads, pins and rings, demonstrating how advanced this Bronze Age community was.

The next phase of building, which probably took place during the Iron Age, included a second wall that follows the curve of the inner wall before extending eastward to take in a considerable area of land until finally halting at the cliff face. Further out are fragments of a third wall that once followed the general outline of the other walls. It is believed that this third wall was demolished in order to provide stone for the building of the fourth wall – a massive structure that extends for four hundred metres and encloses a D-shaped plot.

Between the third and fourth walls are the well-preserved remains of *chevaux-de-frise*. This is an arrangement of closely spaced standing stones, some up to 1.75 metres in height, which slope toward one another, making passage through them slow and difficult. The stones were quarried on site, like those for the fort itself. John O'Donovan of the Ordnance Survey wrote this description of the *chevaux-de-frise* in 1839:

Some of these stones appear at a distance like soldiers making the onset, and many of them are so sharp that if one fell against them they would run him through. This army of stones would appear to have been intended by the Bolgae [Fir Bolg] of Aran to answer the same purpose as the modern *chevaux-de-frise*, now generally used in making a retrenchment to stop cavalry; but these stones were never intended to keep off horses, as no horses could come near the place without 'breaking their legs'. They must have been, therefore, used for keeping off men, and very well adapted they are for this purpose, for a few men standing on the outer wall just described could by casting stones kill hundreds of invaders while attempting to pass through this army of sharp stones.

Even today, after centuries of exposure to the winds and the driving rain, some of these standing stones remain razor-sharp to the touch.

Looking at Dun Aengus, one can only wonder who chose to live in this remote stony monument. We will never know the answer for certain. It suggests dominance by a ruling dynasty and may have been used for great community gatherings in its earliest phases. Dun Aengus appears to have been lived in and possibly strengthened in Early Christian times.

DÚCATHAIR ON INISHMORE

Dúcathair ('the Black Fort') is situated on a promontory east of Dun Aengus. Here the cliffs are much lower but they guard the fort on three sides, affording it excellent protection. The fort itself consists of a single roughly constructed wall, sixty metres in length, six metres high and over five metres thick. The wall runs across the neck of the promontory, providing an effective and easily defended barrier. The wall, like that at Dun Aengus, rises in two steps, and *chevaux-de-frise* on the landward side combine with the sheer cliffs to make this a secure defensive site. Within the circular enclosure are the remains of oval-shaped stone huts, which would have stood huddled close together.

The massive wall of Dúcathair seen from inside the fortification. In the foreground are the ruins of the stone huts that were the probably dwellings of the original inhabitants.

Dún Eochla.

DÚN EOCHLA ON INISHMORE

Dún Eochla ('the Fort of the Yew Wood') is a well-preserved example of an oval-shaped hill fort. It is situated near to the highest point on Inishmore, commanding a magnificent view of the sea approaches on all sides of the island. It consists of two roughly concentric, massively built walls. The inner enclosure houses a large mound of loose stones, which were accumulated during reconstruction work in the late nineteenth century. These stones are believed to be the last remnants of the *clocháns*, or dry-stone beehive huts, which were formerly occupied by the inhabitants of the *dún*.

DÚN EOGHANACHTA ON INISHMORE

Dún Eoghanachta ('the Fort of the Eoghanacht tribe') takes its name from a Munster clan that is reputed to have occupied part of the island at one time. The fort is situated on the western hill of Inishmore, near to a summit of 108 metres. Excavation evidence suggests it was constructed

95

An aerial view of Dún Eoghanachta.

between AD650 and AD800. It too is a circular hill fort, but it is univallate, that is, it has only one surrounding wall. The wall is constructed of massive blocks of limestone and is five metres high and over four metres thick. The fort was probably the residence of a farming clan group, as it is situated within reach of some relatively good agricultural land. The remains of three stone huts are all that can be seen now of its past days as a defended dwelling site. Dún Eoghanachta overlooks the site that was later chosen for one of the major monasteries of Aran: Na Seacht dTeampaill ('the Seven Temples').

DÚN CHONCHÚIR ON INISHMAAN

Dún Chonchúir ('Conor's Fort') occupies a splendid site on the northern side of the highest summit on the island. The enclosure is oval in shape and is surrounded by a wall up to six metres high and five metres thick;

An aerial view over Inishmaan shows the remarkable Dún Chonchúir (Conor's Fort).

thousands of tonnes of stone went into the building of the walls. As at the other forts, the wall has a wide base and rises in two steps so that it is much narrower at the top. There is a semi-circular outer wall, but it does not extend to the southern or western sides of the inner circle; a steep rocky slope on these sides probably convinced the dún-builders that the natural defences were already adequate. At the northernmost corner of this outer wall, there is a small walled enclosure that may have acted as a defended gateway. Within the fort are the remains of a number of stone-built structures, which may have been clocháns.

The last person to dwell in the fort, however, was neither a farmer nor a chieftain. A mainland man named Malley was the last resident, in dubious circumstances. He had accidentally killed his father in a fit of anger, and he sought refuge on Aran. The islanders hid him in a crevice in the wall of the fort for several months, until he managed to make good his escape to America. This incident, reputed to have occurred sometime during the nineteenth century, was related to J.M. Synge during one of his sojourns on Aran. The playwright was much taken with the story and later used it as the inspiration for the plot of his famous comedy, *The Playboy of the Western World*.

The land around Dún Chonchúir is among the best available on Inishmaan, and many of the island farmers own fields in the vicinity of the fort. From the topmost rampart one can see how the fields, with their maze of stone walls, follow the lines of the fortification.

DÚN FHEARBHAIGH ON INISHMAAN

This single-walled fort, known as Dún Fhearbhaigh or Dún Moher, is less impressive than Dún Chonchúir. It is smaller in size and different in shape from the other forts, being a D-shaped, almost square structure. It, too, is situated in good farmland, overlooking the area of Baile an Mhothair, and was probably the dwelling place of a tribal farming group.

DÚN FORMNA ON INISHEER

The hilltop fort of Dún Formna is situated near to the highest point on Inisheer, occupying a commanding position on the northern side of the island, overlooking the harbour. Only one wall of this fort has survived and although considerable in its extent, it is less massive in its construction than the other forts. In the fourteenth or fifteenth century,

Dún Formna and O'Brien's Castle.

the O'Brien clan of County Clare, who ruled the Aran Islands at that time, built a tower house, or castle, within the enclosure of Dún Formna, known as Caisleán Uí Bhriain ('O'Brien's Castle'). This two-storey castle probably utilised the old line of the dún as an outer defensive barrier. On the outer stonework of the castle, there are two projecting corbels worth examining. They are carved roughly with human faces, although the purpose and meaning of these oddities is unknown.

Above: Na Seacht dTeampaill ('the Seven Churches') on Inishmore. All that remain now are the substantial ruins of two churches and a number of domestic buildings.
Below: Clochán na Carraige on Inishmore, one of the best examples of a dry-stone beehive hut in Ireland, dating from the early Christian period.

CHAPTER SIX

ISLANDS OF SAINTS
AND PILGRIMS

Aran has a long reputation as a blessed place and a site of pilgrimage. As early as the sixth century, holy men and women were drawn to Aran's otherworldly wildness, its remote tranquillity and its demanding environment. Monasteries were founded on all three islands, and Aran's fame grew as scholars and pilgrims made the journey to its shores. Today, there are many, many remains from the heyday of its religious activity, causing Aran to be known far and wide as Ára na Naomh – 'the Island of Saints'.

A typical monastery in Early Christian Ireland would have centred on a group of small churches. The monks would have lived in cells nearby, which on Aran would have been the dry-stone beehive huts called clocháns. The monastery would also have had workshops for blacksmiths and scribes, and perhaps a building to house visitors. Many of the monasteries also had schools, which attracted students from Britain and Europe. Some of the monks worked as scribes, copying the Gospels by hand onto vellum (sheets of cured calf-hide). The monks also compiled annals, recording the important events that occurred in the locality each year. Manuscripts of this kind were almost certainly compiled on Aran, but none has survived.

The monastery farm would have provided for all the needs of the community. The monks grew corn, which they milled by hand to make bread. They kept herds of cattle and sheep, and in some cases chickens and bees. When possible, fish from the lakes and the sea was part of their diet.

The whole monastic settlement would have been surrounded by an earthen bank, or a stone wall, and the perimeter of the site was usually marked by stone crosses. At first these crosses were cut into the face of any convenient boulder, but later the stone was hewn into the shape of a cross. As the skill of the stone-cutters developed over the centuries, they began to decorate the crosses with elaborate designs and lettering. Many magnificent examples of these High Crosses can still be seen elsewhere in Ireland; fine examples are found at Clonmacnoise and Monasterboice.

INISHMORE: SAINT ENDA & KILLEANY

Christianity is believed to have been brought to Aran by St Enda, who founded a monastery at Killeany (*Cill Éinne*) on Inishmore in AD490. Now revered as the patron saint of Aran, Enda is said to have been miraculously transported over the waves to Aran in a stone boat, coming to land near Killeany, where he set about building one of the most influential monasteries of the age. The name Cill Éinne means, literally, 'the church of Enda'.

Enda's foundation was one of the earliest and most important Irish monasteries of the period. It became famous, and holy men flocked there to lead a life of study and prayer. Enda's disciples followed a strict rule

Portions of a cross shaft that have been cemented together on the site of Enda's monastery. The intricate carving was typical of the high crosses of the period.

of asceticism and hard work, devoting their lives entirely to God and the monastic community. Many of those who trained under Enda's rule later founded monasteries of their own elsewhere in Ireland or on the Continent, men such as Ciarán of Clonmacnoise, Jarlath of Tuam, Colmcille of Iona and Brendan of Clonfert.

Ruins on the edge of An Trá Mór ('the Great Strand'), at the eastern end of Inishmore, mark the place where Enda settled with his monks. The two small stone churches (Teaghlach Éinne and Teampall Bheanáin), the stump of a once lofty round tower, and fragments of two inscribed stone crosses are all later replacements and additions to the early foundation. The site originally had six churches, but Cromwellian soldiers demolished the other four buildings in the seventeenth century to provide building material for Arkyne Castle (*Caisleán Aircín*) near Killeany harbour. Teaghlach Éinne and Teampall Bheanáin probably stood apart from the main monastery and were therefore saved from destruction.

Teaghlach Éinne is a simple church, possibly dating to the ninth century. It stands within an ancient graveyard among the sand dunes at the

Teampall Bheanáin, the tiny hilltop church dedicated to St. Benan.

east end of An Trá Mór. This graveyard is reputed to be the burial site of Enda and over a hundred of his followers, and it still serves as a cemetery for the people of nearby villages. Some of the inscriptions are just about legible and call up the names of people long since forgotten. One asks the visitor to pray for Scandlan (*Oroit ar Scandlan*), while another is inscribed with a message in Latin and Irish: *Bend die f an Scan* (*Bendacht die for ainm Scanctan)*, meaning 'the blessing of God on the soul of Sanctan'.

Teampall Bheanáin, thought to date to the eleventh century, overlooks the bay from a remarkable hilltop position. It is a tiny church, hardly 4.5 metres in its internal length, and is constructed from massive stone slabs. Regarded as the smallest church in Europe, it is oriented from north to south, in contrast with all the other Aran churches, which are oriented east to west. Nearby are the ruins of a number of clocháns, or beehive huts, and the remnant of a wall, which might once have surrounded the settlement.

The stump of a round tower can be seen in a field near the sheltered harbour. This tower is said to have been sixty metres high and to have blown down in a storm in the late seventeenth century. Elaborately carved sections of the shaft of a cross, which were found near this site, stand in a field to the east of the tower. There is also a holy well, Tobar Éinne ('Enda's Well'), which is roofed by a stone slab. Next to it is a roughly built altar with a cross slab.

Many legends concerning miraculous events in the life of Enda are still related. One such story from the island's folklore concerns the visit of St Colmcille to Cill Éinne. Colmcille loved the peace and beauty of Aran, so he asked Enda for a plot of ground on which he might build

a cell. Enda refused, fearing that Colmcille's fame would overshadow his own. Colmcille eventually persuaded Enda to let him take just as much land as his cloak would cover. But when the cloak was spread on the ground, it began to grow, and Enda snatched it up lest it cover the whole of his island. Colmcille became violently angry and laid a curse on the island that

Teampall Bheanáin overlooks the bay from a remarkable hilltop position over An Trá Mór at the eastern end of Inishmore.

was never to be lifted. He declared that strangers and foreigners would overrun the islands; that the land would not yield a harvest without great labour; that the cows would not produce milk in great quantity; and that turf would never be found there. Enda's greatest fear also came to pass, for a greater devotion exists to St Colmcille on the islands than to any other saint.

Enda's monastery flourished for over five hundred years after his death. Indeed, the period from the seventh to the tenth century is known as Aran's Golden Age, due to the volume of religious activity that was ongoing at that time. Monks from this foundation were found preaching the Gospel in all parts of Europe during the Dark Ages. In the eleventh century, the monastery suffered a succession of disasters. It was almost destroyed by fire in 1020, and was raided by Vikings in 1017 and again in 1081. In time, the community became apathetic and its rule lax, until the arrival of Franciscan monks in the fifteenth century. The last recorded abbot of Cill Éinne died in 1400, but the monastery seems to have lived on. It survived the reign of King Henry VIII, when most of the Irish monasteries were suppressed, and continued its work until 1586, when it, too, was finally dissolved by his daughter, Queen Elizabeth I.

INISMORE: EOGHANACHT

The second greatest monastic settlement on Inishmore is known as Na Seacht dTeampaill ('the Seven Churches'), and it is found near the village of Eoghanacht in the western part of the island. It is uncertain whether there were ever seven churches on this site, for all that now remains are the substantial ruins of two churches and a number of domestic buildings. This monastery, like that at Killeany, occupies good

Only two churches remain at the site of Na Seacht dTeampaill ('the Seven Churches') in the western part of Inishmore.

IN LOVING MEMORY OF
PATRICK FLAHERTY
DIED 11 OCT 1966 AGED 74 YEARS
HIS BROTHER MICHAEL
DIED 30 1 1992 AGED 84 YRS

Teampall a'Phoill, the Church of the Hollow.

land with a permanent supply of fresh water: a stream runs through the little valley where it is located, and some of the deepest soil on Inishmore can be found here.

The older of the two extant churches dates from the eighth century and is dedicated to St Brecan. When first built, Teampall Bhreacáin was similar in size to Teaghlach Éinne, but it was enlarged over the centuries; the west gable clearly shows the original dimensions. St Brecan was renowned for his piety and for the severity of his rule, but little is known of the details of his life. He is said to have arrived on Aran in the fifth or early sixth century, to have been a monk in the Cill Éinne community, and to have succeeded Enda as abbot. A legend has attached to Brecan, based on a poem he wrote to commemorate his arrival on the island. He describes a fantastical scene with a devil he called 'Fierce Brecan Clairingneach', whom he claims to have expelled before appropriating his name and land for the purpose of God's work.

Whatever the truth of his arrival on Aran, once there, Brecan founded a complex that was probably a place of pilgrimage, as suggested by the remains of holy wells, high crosses and inscribed grave slabs. One of these slabs bears the inscription *Sci Brecani*, with *Sci* being an abbreviation of *Sancti*, suggesting that this could be Leaba Bhreacáin ('Brechan's Bed') – the final resting place of the saint. Northeast of the church are the remains of a high cross that must have been very impressive – originally it stood over four metres high and was made from one single massive limestone slab.

The second church at Brecan's site, Teampall a'Phoill ('the Church of the Hollow'), is situated a few metres further up the valley. It is a fifteenth-century structure, which was probably used as an ordinary parish church until relatively recent times. Located near these churches are the remains of five rectangular domestic buildings. They date from various periods, and some were built as late as the sixteenth century.

A highly decorated standing stone at Na Seacht dTeampaill.

Teampall MacDuach on Inishmore. The very fine medieval arch was part of an extension in the Romanesque style.

Between the two major sites at Cill Éinne and Eoghanacht are the ruins of numerous other Early Christian buildings. The most notable of these is Teampall an Ceathrar Álainn ('the Church of the Four Beautiful Ones'), situated south of the main road near the village of Cowrugh (Corrúch). The four saints alluded to are Fursey, Brendan, Conall and Berchan. There are no records to explain why the church is dedicated to these saints, nor do we know why they were described as 'the Four Beautiful Ones'.

South of this church, in a nearby field, is a holy well protected by a low stone wall. Like all holy wells, this was reputed to be blessed, and people believed its waters could cure blindness and epilepsy. While staying on the island, J.M. Synge heard the story of a blind young man from Sligo who regained his sight at this well. Synge used this story in his play *The Well of the Saints*.

Teampall MacDuach, near Kilmurvey, is dedicated to Colmán Mac Duach, patron saint of sailors. The church is probably an eleventh-century building. A well dedicated to St Colman is located nearby. On the north wall of the church is a curious carving of an animal, although there is no agreement as to which animal is represented – some believe it is a horse, others a fox, others a pine-marten. Teampall na Naomh, the Church of the Saints, is also situated near Kilmurvey, but little or nothing is known about it.

In the district of Mainistir, about a kilometre and a half west of Kilronan, is Teampall Chiaráin ('Ciaran's Temple'), a church that originated in the Early Christian era and was enlarged to its present substantial size in the medieval period. Tobar Chiaráin ('Ciaran's Well') is located west of the church. St Ciarán, a disciple of Enda's, is believed to have founded this site in the sixth century, prior to establishing one of the greatest monasteries in Ireland: Clonmacnoise. The nearest sea inlet to Ciarán's site is Port na Mainistreach, or 'the Bay of the Monastery'. There is an *atharla*, or burial place, located on a small hill overlooking this bay. The locals know this as unsanctified ground – a burial place where unbaptised children were interred, a practice common until recent times. Several stones protrude from the grass; all that is left of whoever was laid to rest here.

Some distance west of Teampall Chiaráin is the much smaller Teampall Asurnai, thought to be dedicated to a female saint, Soarney, though this is in no way certain. To the east of the church is a stone believed to mark St Soarney's grave. There is also a thorn tree held sacred to her name – a common feature at pilgrimage sites.

INISHMAAN

Inishmaan seems never to have supported a major monastic community, though a complex of ruins exists on fertile land near the centre of the island, which indicates that a monastery may once have occupied the site. Teampall na Seacht Mac Rí, of which only the foundations remain, commemorates seven brothers of noble birth who came here as hermits. Nearby is Atharla Chinndeirge and Tobar Chinndeirge, the burial place and holy well of a female saint. Also in this area, Teampall Mhuire is a late medieval building, probably built in the fifteenth century, that served as a parish church for over five hundred years.

Near the eastern shore of this island stands the well-preserved remains

The shifting sand dunes of Inisheer are believed to have buried a number of ancient settlements. Teampall Chaomháin has escaped the same fate because the sand is shovelled out of the building each year on 14 June, the saint's birthday.

of a small church known as Cill Cheannannach. The derivation of the name is not now known – presumably Ceannannach was a saint – but we do know that the site was founded by Ultan, a renowned scribe. The church itself is a simple structure, but there are some interesting features on the site. Tobar Cheannannach lies northwest of the church, and there are fifteenth-, nineteenth- and twentieth-century grave slabs here. An end-stone of what would once have been a stone-built reliquary can also be seen. Such reliquaries were built to house relics, such as the bones of a holy person. A shrine of this kind can be seen at the little site of Cill Comhla on Inishmore, north of Dún Eoghanachta. Sometimes the end stone has a hole in it – as this one at Cill Cheannannach does – to allow the pilgrim to reach in and touch the holy relic.

INISHEER

On Inisheer the remains of several churches can be seen, though tradition maintains that others have been swallowed up by the shifting sand dunes at the northern end of the island. South of O'Brien's Castle, at Ceathrú an Chaisleáin, some traces of the foundations of a church, Cill na Seacht nIníon ('the Church of the Seven Daughters'), can be seen. Nothing is known of these seven female saints. Although their identity remains a mystery, we do know that a cult of the seven daughters existed – there are several holy wells in Connemara dedicated to them.

Over on the northern shore, Teampall Chaomháin ('the Church of St Cavan') is well preserved. It stands in a burial ground among the sand dunes and is in constant danger of being covered completely by the movement of the sands. It appears to be struggling to rise up from a cavern of sand, encroached upon and half-buried as it is by the blown sand that has built up on every side. St Cavan is believed to have been a brother of St Kevin of Glendalough. A considerable devotion to him still exists on Inisheer, and Cavan remains a common Christian name for boys on the island. Near the church a horizontal grave slab, ornately carved, is said to be Leaba Chiaráin, Ciaran's burial place.

Cill Ghobnait ('the Church of St Gobnet'), another small church, is dedicated to a female saint who is venerated in Munster and who found refuge for a time on Inisheer. The church was probably built in the eleventh century in honour of Gobnet, the patron saint of beekeepers. The site has the remains of a clochán, gravestones and bullaun stones, along with a well dedicated to St Enda.

THE *TURAS* AND SAINT LORE

The lives of the saints and the various remnants of their time on Aran are held sacred by Christians, and a curious mix of pagan and Christian traditions has grown up around the worship of saints. The superstitious belief that the water in holy wells has curative properties, or that certain trees should be revered, stem from pagan times and rituals. One of the most common of these folk beliefs is that spending a night lying on a saint's *leaba*, or gravestone, will cure various ailments. The islanders can provide many a tale to prove the truth of this ancient panacea.

In Ireland, the *patrún* (pattern) or *turas* (pilgrimage) is an important way to commemorate a saint on his or her feast day. This involves going to a place associated with the saint and walking around the site whilst reciting prayers. It takes place in complete silence and is often accompanied by a ritual gesture; for example, walking around the site seven times and casting down a stone upon the completion of each circuit.

On Inishmore, a *patrún* festival still takes place each year on 29 June to mark the feast days of saints Peter and Paul, who are closely associated with Na Seacht dTeampaill. In past times the islanders would have made a pilgrimage to the monastic site, but nowadays they gather in Kilronan for a three-day celebration involving Mass, games, competitions and the ever-popular tug-o'-war and currach race.

Other important dates observed on Aran are: 9 June, turas at Killeany in honour of Colmcille; 14 June, turas on Inisheer for St Cavan's feast day; 15 August, turas in honour of the Assumption; and 9 September, turas in honour of St Ciaran.

ON ARRAN ISLAND GALWAY 5055 W.L.

CHAPTER SEVEN

A FINAL FAREWELL

One of the most common experiences through the ages for Aran Island dwellers is, of course, emigration, especially through the nineteenth and twentieth centuries. Before flying was a common and affordable experience, leaving the islands was a final farewell with little or no chance of visiting home again. The event was marked by the 'American wake', which was like a funeral. Many Aran Islanders went straight from the wildness of the islands to the heart of Boston or New York or other American cities.

In the following extract from his short story 'Going into Exile', Aran Island writer Liam O'Flaherty describes the departure, a sad occasion for all involved but especially the parents of those leaving.

Mary and Michael got to their feet. The father sprinkled them with holy water and they crossed themselves. Then, without looking at their mother, who lay in the chair with her hands clasped on her lap, looking at the ground in a silent, tearless stupor, they left the room.

Each hurriedly kissed little Thomas, who was not going to Kilmurrage, and then, hand in hand, they left the house. As Michael was going out the door he picked a piece of loose whitewash from the wall and put it in his pocket. The people filed out after them, down the yard and on to the road, like a funeral procession. The mother was left in the house with little Thomas and two old peasant women from the village. Nobody spoke in the cabin for a very long time.

Then the mother rose and came into the kitchen. She looked at the two women, at her little son and at the hearth, as if she were looking for something she had lost. Then she threw her hands into the air and ran out into the yard.

'Come back,' she screamed; 'come back to me.'

She looked wildly down the road with dilated nostrils, her bosom heaving. But there was nobody in sight. Nobody replied. There was a crooked stretch of limestone road, surrounded by grey crags that were scorched by the sun. The road ended in a hill and then dropped out of sight. The hot June day was silent. Listening foolishly for an answering cry, the mother imagined she could hear the crags simmering under the hot rays of the sun. It was something in her head that was singing.

The two old women led her back into the kitchen. 'There is nothing that time will not cure,' said one. 'Yes. Time and patience,' said the other.

PRACTICAL INFORMATION

GETTING THERE

You can travel to the Aran Islands by sea (passengers only) or by air. The ferry from Rossaveal in County Galway runs all year round, while travel from Doolin in County Clare is from spring to autumn only. Flights and ferries stop at all three of the main islands: Inishmore, Inishmaan and Inisheer.

FERRIES

Aran Island Ferries travel from Rossaveal (c. 40km from Galway city; shuttle bus available) to each of the three islands, every day and all year around. *www.aranislandferries.com*

A number of companies (some linked) operate between Doolin in County Clare (c. 65km from Shannon Airport) and the three islands between March and November. Bookings can be made online or at the pier in Doolin.

O'Brien Line: *www.obrienline.com*
Doolin Ferry: *www.doolinferry.com*
Doolin2Aran Ferries: *www.doolin2aranferries.com*
Doolin Ferries: *www.doolinferries.com*

FLIGHTS

Aer Arann Islands provides a daily Air Taxi service from Connemara Airport in Inverin, County Galway (c. 30km from Galway city), to each of the three islands. A single ticket costs around €25, with reductions for islanders, students, children and groups. *www.aerarannislands.ie*

GETTING AROUND

There isn't a dedicated car ferry that travels to Aran, so the few vehicles you'll see on the roads belong to the locals. Many visitors choose to cycle around the islands; you can hire bikes from vendors near each of the ferry ports.

You can also explore on foot – the islands are generally quite flat but rocky, so strong shoes or hiking boots are recommended. You'll find routes and maps online or at the tourist office (details below).

Alternatively, you can take a mini-bus or taxi tour – or even a pony-and-trap ride – with a local guide. Although offered on all three islands, these services are easier to come across on Inisheer and particularly Inishmore.

TOURIST INFORMATION

The **Aran Islands Tourist Office** is located in Kilronan, Inishmore, just opposite the pier. It is open office hours, seven days a week, all year round. **Ionad Arann**, Aran's Heritage Centre, is a few minutes' walk from the centre of Kilronan, at the back of the old coastguard station.

Also available from
The O'Brien Press

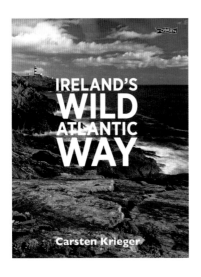

Ireland's Wild Atlantic Way
By Carsten Krieger

Take a photographic journey along the Wild Atlantic Way, from Donegal in the north to Cork in the south, with this sumptuous book full of photographs, maps, and evocative quotations about the west coast of Ireland. Also available in German.

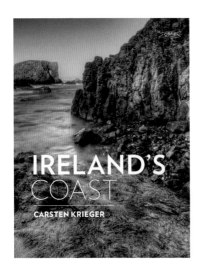

Ireland's Coast
By Carsten Krieger

A stunning collection of photographs showcasing Ireland's coastal landscape, wildlife and people, interspersed with stories and anecdotes compiled over the author's two years of travel. Perfect for both native and visitor.

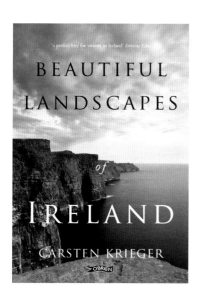

**Beautiful Landscapes
of Ireland**
By Carsten Krieger

From Glendalough to the
Giant's Causeway, the Burren
to the Skelligs, this atmospheric
collection of photographs shows
the beauty and diversity of
Ireland's landscape.

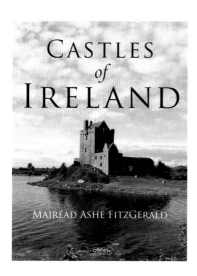

Castles of Ireland
By Mairéad Ashe FitzGerald

The romantic appearance of
Ireland's castles belies their
turbulent past, their stories
of sieges, betrayals and daring
escapes. This book visits more
than sixty castles, many of which
played an important role in
Ireland's history.

www.obrien.ie

Also available from
The O'Brien Press

Let's See Ireland
By Sarah Bowie

Take a journey with Molly around the whole of Ireland in this gorgeous picture book that is sure to delight adults and children alike!

Where's Larry?
Where's Larry This Time?
By Philip Barrett

Follow Larry the Leprechaun around Ireland and see if you can find him in Newgrange, at the Rock of Cashel, in Belfast, in the Skelligs, or in the St. Patrick's Day Parade in Dublin! Great fun for all the family.

My Ireland Activity Books: The Wild Atlantic Way, Cliffs of Moher & the Burren
By Natasha Mac a'Bháird and Alan Nolan

Bright and fun-filled activity books set on the wild west coast of Ireland. Puzzles, games, colouring, stories and tons of interesting facts.

A Dublin Fairytale
By Nicola Colton

Fiona's on her way to Granny's house … but who's following her through the streets of Dublin? Join Fiona and her friends as they visit some of the city's most famous landmarks and locations in this modern Dublin fairytale.

www.obrien.ie

ACKNOWLEDGEMENTS

The publisher would like to thank Ann Jackson and Brian Kavanagh for work in the development of the materials; Tim O'Neill for reading and commenting on the manuscript; Mr Seamus Heaney for 'The Evening Land', 'Inisheer' and 'The Oarsman's Song'; Jonathan Cape Ltd for 'Going into Exile' from *The Short Stories of Liam O'Flaherty*; extracts from *The Islandman* by Tomás Ó Crohan, by permission of the Oxford University Press; for 'Thatcher' reprinted by permission of Faber and Faber Ltd., from *Door into the Dark* by Seamus Heaney. In instances where we failed to trace the copyright holder, we would be grateful if they would contact the publisher. The publisher also wishes to thank the following for their help in preparing the 2003 edition of this book: Mairéad Ashe FitzGerald, Paul Walsh, the staff at Cill Rónáin Heritage Centre, George Munday, Colman Doyle, Emma Byrne and Rachel Pierce.

The authors and publisher thank the following for permission to use photographs and illustrative material: front cover, back cover (bottom), pp. 8, 11, 12, 17, 20, 21, 22, 27, 29, 31, 36, 41, 50, 51, 52, 53 (both), 64, 66 (both), 68, 69, 71, 72, 74, 80–81, 89 (both), 90, 95, 100 (both), 104, 105, 107, 115, 119 and 122–123 courtesy of Shutterstock; pp. 1 and 99: images sourced from Failte Ireland and Tourism Ireland; pp. 2–3 and 112 courtesy of Brian Morrison Photography; back cover (top left), pp. 4–5, 82 and 97 courtesy of Chris Hill at scenicireland.com; pp. 85, 92 and 96 courtesy of Aircam Ireland; p.26 courtesy of Red Bull; pp. 19, 24, 28, 30, 34, 38, 42, 49 and 103 courtesy of the National Museum of Ireland; back cover (top right), pp. 14, 32, 36, 43, 45, 46 (both) 59, 62, 76 and 84 courtesy of Pat Langan and *The Irish Times*; pp. 43, 73 and 116 courtesy of the National Library of Ireland; pp. 14, 39, 61, 86, 91, 94, 108 and 109 courtesy of Bord Failte. Every effort has been made to contact the copyright holders for all pictures. If any omission or oversight has occurred we would request the copyright holder(s) to inform the publisher.